Importing Core International Crimes into National Law

Morten Bergsmo, Mads Harlem and Nobuo Hayashi
(editors)

2010
Second Edition
Torkel Opsahl Academic EPublisher
Oslo

This and other books in the FICHL Publication Series may be openly accessed and downloaded through the Forum website (www.fichl.org). Printed copies may be ordered at www.amazon.co.uk. This book was first published 12 July 2007. The Second Edition was published 19 April 2010.

ISBN 978-82-93081-00-5

PREFACE TO THE SECOND EDITION

The text of this second edition of Importing Core International Crimes into National Law has undergone only minor editorial changes. It is published as one of the first volumes released by the Torkel Opsahl Academic EPublisher as part of the broadening open access platform of the Forum for International Criminal and Humanitarian Law. It can be freely read, printed and downloaded from the Forum Internet site (www.fichl.org). But it can also be purchased through Amazon as a regular book. Firmly committed to open access, the Forum and EPublisher do not charge for these authorized printed versions of their books. The printer and Amazon do however charge for their production and distribution costs.

Morten Bergsmo
Series Co-Editor

Alf Butenschøn Skre
Senior Editorial Assistant

PREFACE BY THE SERIES EDITOR

We started the *Forum for International Criminal Justice and Conflict*[1] as a debate forum open to individuals interested in issues concerning international criminal justice and conflict, with the main aim to identify, and facilitate debate on, key issues in international criminal justice and conflict, including accountability-related measures other than criminal justice. The process to import the core international crimes of genocide, crimes against humanity and war crimes into national criminal law is an issue of critical importance to the emerging system of international criminal justice. The architecture of this system rests on the principle of complementarity, which provides that the International Criminal Court may have to investigate and prosecute cases that are not dealt with genuinely by national criminal justice systems. This entails a two-fold requirement of national preparedness to deal with core international crimes.

First, states should have some *institutional* capacity to investigate and prosecute genocide, crimes against humanity and war crimes cases within the national jurisdiction. If there are insufficient resources to have a separate unit for such crimes, then the state should facilitate that some members of the criminal justice system develop expertise in this area through suitable competence building measures, including training and access to specialized electronic resources.

Secondly, states should develop *legislative* capacity to prosecute and adjudicate core international crimes cases before national courts. This includes provisions in national criminal law explicitly criminalising genocide, crimes against humanity and war crimes. Without such offences in national criminal law it may not be possible to bring cases with the proper international legal classification, forcing prosecutors and judges to fall back on ordinary national crimes which may not

[1] The Forum was later renamed to "Forum for International Criminal and Humanitarian Law".

adequately capture the interests that are protected by the core international crimes.

The *Forum* held an international seminar in Oslo on 27 October 2006 at the initiative of the Norwegian Red Cross and PRIO to discuss different aspects of the import of core international crimes into national criminal law. The present publication gives a broader audience access to the deliberations at the seminar, in the form of the first issue in the *FICJC Publications* series.

Morten Bergsmo
Series Editor

PREFACE BY THE EDITORS

The 27 October 2006 seminar on importing core international crimes into national criminal law was held, *inter alia*, with a view to raising awareness and momentum in Norway as it prepared to adopt a new penal code. This publication records the proceedings of the event.

The half-day seminar opened with a review of the various approaches and techniques available to national legislators. It then examined the experience of Canada and Germany in incorporating war crimes, crimes against humanity and genocide, including those found in the Rome Statute of the International Criminal Court (ICC), into their penal law. At the plenary, the relevance of the ICC Elements of Crimes document and the treatment of crimes excluded from the ICC Statute became the subject of in-depth discussion.

The seminar attracted numerous participants from Norway and beyond. Their diverse backgrounds – for example, students, scholars, prosecutors, private practitioners, members of the judiciary and ministerial staffers – contributed to the lively and constructive exchange of ideas. Above all, those present benefited from the expert speakers and panellists with backgrounds in Canada, Germany, Norway and Sweden as well as in the international arena.

This publication contains (a) the final programme, (b) the minutes of the proceedings, (c) a supplementary article by one of the panellists at the plenary, and (d) the English text of the implementing legislations adopted in Canada and Germany. Nobuo Hayashi has edited the minutes of the proceedings in co-operation with the speakers. Despite the primarily Norwegian context in which the seminar took place, its content, as summarised in the following pages, would be of interest to States concerned with ICC national implementation and to those active in the administration of international criminal justice generally.

Special acknowledgement is due to the rapporteurs for their diligent note-taking and for preparing the minutes; the Norwegian Red Cross for providing the rapporteurs with audio-recording assistance;

the speakers and panellists for their feedback on earlier drafts of the minutes; and PRIO Information Director Agnete Schjønsby for designing, formatting and printing of the First Edition of this publication.

Morten Bergsmo
Nobuo Hayashi
Mads Harlem
Editors

TABLE OF CONTENTS

MINUTES OF THE PROCEEDINGS

Final Seminar Programme

12:00 *Introduction*, by Trygve Nordby (Secretary-General, Norwegian Red Cross).

12:10 *Overview of ways to import core international crimes into national criminal law*, by Stéphane J. Hankins[1] (Legal Adviser, International Committee of the Red Cross).

12:40 *The Canadian model*, by Joseph Rikhof[2] (Senior Counsel, Crimes against Humanity and War Crimes Section, Canadian Department of Justice).

13:10 *The German model*, by Professor Claus Kreß[3] (Professor, University of Cologne).

---

1 **Stéphane J. Hankins** is a graduate from the Law Faculty of the University of Paris I (Panthéon Sorbonne) and from the Central European University in Prague. He has been working for the International Committee of the Red Cross since 1994 as regional legal adviser based successively in Moscow, Budapest, Bangkok and Kuala-Lumpur. He is currently working with the ICRC Advisory Service on international humanitarian law at ICRC Headquarters in Geneva.

2 **Joseph Rikhof** (BCL, University of Nijmegen, The Netherlands; LL.B, McGill University; Diploma in Air and Space Law, McGill University) teaches the course International Criminal Law at the University of Ottawa. He is Senior Counsel, Manager of the Law with the Crimes against Humanity and War Crimes Section of the Department of Justice, Canada. He has also served as Special Counsel and Policy Advisor to the Modern War Crimes Section of the Department of Citizenship & Immigration between 1998 and 2002. His area of expertise lies in the area of the law related to organized crime, terrorism, genocide, war crimes and crimes against humanity, especially in the context of immigration and refugee law. He has written a number of articles exploring these areas of international criminal law and immigration/refugee law and has lectured on the same topics in Canada, the United States, Europe and the Middle East.

3 **Claus Kreß** (Dr. jur. Cologne; LL.M. Cantab.) is Professor for Criminal Law, Criminal Procedure, International Criminal Law and Public International Law. He is Director of the Institute for Criminal Law and Criminal Procedure at Cologne

13:40 Break.

14:00 *Discussion on particular problems in connection with the import of core international crimes into national criminal law*, including (but not necessarily limited to):

(a) Role of the ICC Elements of Crime document (with a short introduction by Joseph Rikhof);

(b) Modifying elements of crimes when importing core international crimes (Håkan Friman, Deputy Head of Division, Swedish Ministry of Justice); and

(c) War crimes not included in the ICC Statute (Mads Harlem, Legal Adviser, Norwegian Red Cross).

15:45 *Conclusion*, by Tørris Jæger (Head, International Humanitarian Law Unit, Norwegian Red Cross).

University where he holds the Chair for Criminal Law, Criminal Procedure, European Criminal Law and International Criminal Law. His writings cover most areas of international criminal law and procedure. His prior practice was in the German Federal Ministry of Justice on matters of criminal law and international law. Since 1998 he represents Germany in the negotiations regarding the International Criminal Court. He was member of the Expert Group on the German Code of Crimes under International Law (2000/2001). He acted as War Crimes Expert for the Prosecutor General for East Timor (2001) and as Head of the ICC's Drafting Committee for the Regulations of the Court (2004).

Minutes of the Proceedings

Prepared by (shown in alphabetical order)*:

Cristine M. Delany, Masters student, Norwegian Centre for Human Rights
Yassin Kaarshe, Faculty of Law, University of Oslo
Andreas Kiaby, Masters student, Norwegian Centre for Human Rights
Andreas M. Kravik, Research Assistant, Norwegian Centre for Human Rights
Vibeke Musæus, Student, Faculty of Law, University of Oslo
Ingvild Dønnem Søyseth, Research Assistant, Norwegian Centre for Human Rights
Ellen Stensrud, Research Fellow, Faculty of Social Sciences, University of Oslo

Compiled and edited by:

Nobuo Hayashi, Legal Advisor, Norwegian Centre for Human Rights

* Professional titles as per October 2006.

I

Introduction

The seminar opened with remarks by Trygve Nordby, Secretary General of the Norwegian Red Cross. He noted that, for the first time in human history, a universal international criminal court was established in 1998. The Rome Statute confers upon the ICC jurisdiction over the gravest crimes affecting the entire human kind, namely genocide, crimes against humanity and war crimes.

In Kofi Annan's words, there can be no healing without peace, there can be no peace without justice, and there can be no justice without respect for human rights and the rule of law. Justice is an important tool to a lasting peace, and the ICC is an important tool in fighting impunity for the most serious crimes of concern to the international community.

The ICC cannot and should not, however, play this role alone. Ensuring justice is, first and foremost, the responsibility of national courts. For the purposes of a lasting peace, it is crucial that justice take place as close as possible to the place where the crime was committed. States are therefore obligated to exercise their criminal jurisdiction over those responsible for international crimes. The purpose of this seminar is to discuss particular challenges confronting States in their efforts to import core international crimes into their national criminal law.

Nordby highlighted two issues in this regard. First, should national criminal law adopt separate penal provisions for war crimes, crimes against humanity and genocide? It would not be sufficient to criminalise these offences in accordance with the provisions contained in the penal code relating to homicide. As stated by the Appeals Chamber of the International Criminal Tribunal for Rwanda (ICTR), the criminalisation of genocide, unlike that of homicide, is designed to protect a national, ethnical, racial or religious group as such, rather than individuals. There should therefore be specific provisions relating to genocide, crimes against humanity and war crimes in national legislation.

Second, what should constitute war crimes, crimes against humanity or genocide in national legislation? Norway is in the process of drafting a new penal code. Encouragingly, its penal code commission has considered how the penal provisions of the Rome Statute can be incorporated into Norwegian law. Nonetheless, Norway's obligations go beyond the Rome Statute. National penal provisions relating to genocide, crimes against humanity and war crimes should comply not only with the Rome Statute but also with other parts of international law, such as conventions prohibiting the use of certain weapons in armed conflict. The Norwegian government is currently taking an international initiative to regulate the use and ban certain types of cluster bombs, as it did together with non-governmental and other governmental actors some ten to fifteen years ago to ban anti-personnel mines.

The seminar was chaired by Arne Willy Dahl, Judge Advocate General of Norway.

II

Overview of Ways to Import Core International Crimes into National Criminal Law[1]

A. Introduction

Stéphane J. Hankins, Legal Advisor for the International Committee of the Red Cross, began his presentation by emphasising its focus on the subject-matter jurisdiction of the ICC and its implications in the national legislation of States Parties.

Hankins recalled that the Rome Statute does not directly obligate its States Parties to incorporate core international crimes into their domestic legal order. This remains the case even though the same States may be bound to do so under other obligations resulting from other international treaties to which they are parties and/or customary international law. It was suggested however that the Rome Statute does set forth an *indirect* obligation flowing from the principle of *complementarity* of jurisdiction between the ICC and domestic courts. According to this principle, the ICC is only a court of last resort. If a national court is "able" and "willing" to prosecute a case, that court shall take priority over the ICC. This presupposes that national courts have the necessary legislation in place. States Parties should therefore review their domestic law in order to ensure that it reflects as closely as possible the terms of the Rome Statute, such as the definition of substantive crimes, the gravity of crimes in the definition of applicable penalties and defences against criminal responsibility which should not be broader than those permitted under the Statute.

Hankins referred in this context to the *Bagaragaza* case in which the Appeals Chamber of the ICTR denied a motion by the Prosecution to transfer a case for trial to Norway. It did so on the grounds that Norway lacked the necessary legislation and jurisdiction to try the ac-

[1] This part of the minutes was prepared by Vibeke Musæus.

cused on charges of grave violations of international law including genocide and that in the absence of domestic legislation, the accused could only be charged for ordinary crimes. This, the Chamber decided, risked trivialising the nature and gravity of the crimes in question. This decision, Hankins concluded, while not entirely relevant to the discussion at hand since the ICC is widely expected to show due deference to the jurisdiction of domestic courts unless there is a clear signal that national proceedings are intended to shield an individual from criminal responsibility, was nevertheless very stimulating. It stood as a strong reminder of the gravity of the crimes concerned and of the responsibility for States under international law to create the conditions within their domestic law to investigate and prosecute the gravest international crimes.

Many of the States Parties to the Rome Statute (102 by the end of October 2006) have adopted, or are intending to adopt, legislation introducing the core crimes into their domestic law. Among the wide range of issues the legislator needs to take into consideration are the following:

- Which definitions of the crimes should be adopted (*e.g.* by reference to the definitions and categorisations of the Rome Statute or by drafting specific definitions; by limiting their consideration to the strict implementation of the Rome Statute crimes; or by looking beyond that to other obligations of the State flowing from other relevant international instruments or customary international law)?
- How, and where in domestic law, should the crimes be stipulated (*e.g.*, within a stand-alone legislation or through amendments to existing domestic penal codes)?
- What penalties should be ascribed?
- On what bases should the State assert jurisdiction (for example, jurisdiction on the basis of territoriality and/or nationality, or universal jurisdiction; whether to require the presence of the alleged perpetrator on the national territory; and whether jurisdiction should be asserted retrospectively or only prospectively)?

- Should the existing rules on criminal responsibility be amended in light of the provisions of the Rome Statute?
- How, if at all, should the Elements of Crimes document be used?

B. Methods of reflecting core international crimes in domestic law

Hankins considered a number of ways in which States might define core international crimes within their jurisdictions.

- States may first take the traditional and minimalist approach of *applying existing military or ordinary criminal law* (a method still favoured in several countries, such as Germany prior to the adoption of its Code of Crimes Under International Law of 2002). The disadvantages of this approach are well known. These include the fact that, frequently, the offences concerned correspond only very roughly to the definitions and requirements foreseen under international law and that the penalties provided for in ordinary criminal law may prove inappropriate to the seriousness of international crimes
- Alternatively – and States are increasingly considering to do so in the process of implementing the Rome Statute – core international crimes may be the subject of *express and specific incrimination in domestic law*. Within this approach, once again, Hankins identified different options open to the legislator:
    - The first method of specific incorporation is that of criminalisation through a general and open-ended reference to international treaties to which the State is a Party, to international law in general or to the laws and customs of war, while specifying a range of penalties for the crimes in question. It was suggested, however, that this may prove insufficient with regard to the principle of legality.
    - The second method is to expressly criminalise each and every crime outlined in relevant international treaties and/or recognised under customary international law:

- "Explicit criminalisation" may firstly take the form of a "static" or "literal" transcription, involving a transcription of the offences into domestic law using an identical wording to that of the international treaty, while setting out the penalties applicable to the crimes in question. "Static transcription" accords with the principle of legality because it sets forth clearly and predictably which conduct is considered criminal and what punishment is envisaged therefore. It also facilitates the task of those responsible for applying the law and relieves them of the burden of researching and interpreting international law. It was noted however that such an approach, if the criminalisation is too detailed and specific, may inhibit the ability of domestic courts to prosecute crimes in consideration of new developments in international law. This "static transcription" method is inherent in the approach of common-law States in implementing international treaties, such as England and Wales. Several States of the civil law tradition have also opted for this approach (such as, for example, the recent French draft law to introduce amendments to the Criminal Code and other relevant legislation).
- A second option of "explicit criminalisation" is what may be described as "dynamic transcription", whereby the types of conduct constituting offences under the Rome Statute are redefined, reformulated and redrafted in domestic law. This approach assumes that the Statute definitions and categorisations are not fully consistent with conventional or customary international law. On the one hand, "dynamic transcription" enables the legislator to complement the definitions under the ICC Statute in consideration of the list and wording of crimes in related international instruments, such as Additional Protocol I to the Geneva Conventions of 1949. On the other hand, it may prove a major task for the legislator and entail an extensive review of domestic criminal law.

Germany and the Netherlands, among others, have adopted such an approach albeit to varying degrees.

- A third and last option of "explicit criminalisation" is to combine methods. One mixed approach may combine explicit and specific criminalisation of certain international offences with a generic and residual clause covering, for example, other grave or serious violations of international humanitarian law under treaties to which the State is a party. Finnish criminal law (presently undergoing a reform process) may be considered to typify a mixed approach, in which some core international crimes are expressly defined (the Finnish Criminal Code contains a Chapter 13 on "War Crimes and Crimes against Humanity"), whereas others are incorporated through an open-ended reference to Finland's international obligations (through an express prohibition of any acts which "otherwise violate the provisions of an international agreement on warfare binding upon Finland or the generally acknowledged and established rules and customs of war under public international law"). This mixed approach combines static transcription with dynamic transcription. To put it differently, it combines specific criminalisation with general recourse to relevant international law.

Hankins then examined the form and place of criminalisation. Should the legislator adopt separate enactments covering substantive issues on the one hand and issues related to co-operation with the ICC on the other? Or should one address these matters in a single legislation? Should the crimes be simply inserted into existing penal codes or stipulated separately in a special statute?

Adopting a special, "stand-alone" enactment may notably enable all domestic rules on the implementation of international treaties covering international crimes to be contained in one piece of legislation. This approach also affords an opportunity to bring together under one act both the definition of the crimes and the various general principles of criminal law applicable thereto. In contrast, incorporating international crimes into existing legislation obligates the law-maker to determine the place (for example in ordinary criminal codes, military criminal codes, or both) and the form (for example as a special section or chapter) of their incorporation. Germany, the Netherlands and Canada are among those States which have adopted the special, "stand-alone" approach in implementation of the Rome Statute crimes, whereas France is currently reforming its domestic criminal law (with amendments foreseen to the Criminal Code, the Code of Military Justice and the French Law on the Freedom of the Press, respectively).

Hankins himself did not express any preference for one approach over the other. He did state however that, at any rate, the legislation in place should allow the State to benefit from the *complementarity* principle and enable domestic courts to assert jurisdiction accordingly. States may also be encouraged to adopt a dynamic approach by extending the jurisdiction of domestic courts in order to both account for other related international obligations and remedy some of the omissions or weaknesses in the Rome Statute.

C. Jurisdictional bases for the exercise of national jurisdiction

Hankins proceeded with the discussion of whether States should assert jurisdiction on the basis of *universality* or on a more limited basis such as *territoriality* and *nationality*. It was recalled that the matter remains the subject of much debate and was in recent years brought to renewed attention in the context of high profile cases in the domestic courts of several States (for example Belgium).

Under customary international law, some offences are considered subject to universal jurisdiction. Treaty provisions expressly provide for universal jurisdiction in respect of certain other offences. It was explained that different States have approached the matter in different ways. In Hankins' view, they should take *inter alia* the following factors into consideration:

- Their obligation to assert universal jurisdiction over certain international crimes;

- The principle of complementarity governing the relationship between the ICC Statute and States Parties thereto, as well as the interests of foreign courts in a given case (which may have a greater interest and facility to adjudicate international crimes); and
- The interests of domestic courts in exercising or declining jurisdiction in a given case.

States such as Germany and the Netherlands have hence sought to combine broad extraterritorial jurisdiction over core crimes with a number of procedural safeguards serving to preserve a degree of discretion for domestic prosecutorial and judicial authorities to proceed with in a given case. These arrangements aim to balance respect for the international obligations of the State, for the jurisdiction of other States and for the jurisdiction of international courts.

D. General principles of criminal law

Hankins considered whether the general principles of criminal law in Part 3 of the Rome Statute should be duplicated or otherwise incorporated into domestic law.

The Rome Statute does not directly require the States Parties to adopt the general principles defined therein. Nor does the principle of complementarity dictate that national courts try cases in exactly the same manner or according to exactly the same criteria as the ICC would. Most of the systems considered here, including in particular those of Canada, Germany, the Netherlands and the United Kingdom, indicate that, wherever possible, the general principles of ordinary criminal law should apply to international crimes. It would appear that only certain specific aspects of the general principles need transcription in domestic law. Examples of such aspects include:

- The question of statutes of limitation which may exist in domestic law;
- The question of criminal liability of superiors; and
- The question of immunities of foreign officials.

E. Conclusion

Hankins observed that there is a diversity of approaches to the implementation of core international crimes in the ICC Statute. A key question confronting the legislator is whether to adopt a minimalist approach strictly in keeping with the requirements of the complementarity principle, or a dynamic approach moving beyond the Rome Statute.

III

The Canadian Model[1]

A. Introduction

According to Joseph Rikhof, Senior Counsel and Manager of the Law in the Crimes against Humanity and War Crimes Section of the Department of Justice, Canada, the Canadian model is based on the implementation of international law rather than the amendment of national law by defining crimes in an international context. Historically, Canadian courts have had difficulties in dealing with core crimes. Experiences before these courts in the 1980s and early 1990s have been unsatisfactory. Each criminal case that was taken to court was lost. These problems were partially due to the fact that Canadian judges did not have a great deal of international law experience, combined with evidentiary frailties inherent in cases pertaining to situations fifty years earlier. Canada has since approached international criminal law with a view to giving some clearer indicators in the legislation which could be useful for both prosecutors and national courts.

B. History

Rikhof recalled that, by 1987, Canada had incorporated war crimes and crimes against humanity into its legislation. There have been four World War II-related cases in which an effort was made to link national legislation to international law. This effort was not successful; the Supreme Court of Canada in the *Finta* case in 1994 set the bar for proving international offences so high that it became very difficult to attempt further prosecutions for such crimes. The outcome of the *Finta* case and the demise of the other three cases due to the lack of evidence prompted the Canadian government to amend its Criminal Code in the mid-1990s. When the prospect of an international criminal court became a reality in the late 1990s, the government decided to incorporate

[1] This part of the minutes was prepared by Cristine M. Delaney.

this latest development in international law into its legislation by passing a separate enactment, the Crimes Against Humanity and War Crimes Act of 2000, two years after the adoption of the Rome Statute in 1998. The Act draws heavily on the Rome Statute, while ensuring that some of the more undesirable aspects of the *Finta* case were also addressed.

C. The Crimes Against Humanity and War Crimes Act 2000

The Act marks Canada's first acknowledgement of the crime of genocide. Previously, Canada had incorporated the Genocide Convention only to the extent that *incitement* of genocide was included in the Canadian Criminal Code. The Act also recognised, for the first time, that war crimes can be committed in both international and non-international armed conflicts, while it made superior/command responsibility a specific offense rather than a mode of liability. Canada's earlier recognition of superior/command responsibility was limited to using the concept of aiding and abetting in the commission of war crimes or crimes against humanity.

Prior to 2000, Canadian law distinguished between crimes committed in Canada and those committed outside of Canada. The 1987 legislation only allowed prosecution of the latter. The Act provides for both situations but limits Canada's ability to prosecute core crimes committed within Canada only to acts committed after 2000; it does not, however, impose any such temporal limitations regarding crimes committed in other countries. Any offence committed outside Canada before 2000 can be prosecuted, as long as it constituted an offence under Canadian or international law or was criminal according to the general principles of law recognised by the community of nations at the time of its commission. This exception to the legality/non-retroactivity principle and to the legal rights of accused persons is specifically stated in the Canadian Charter of Rights and Freedoms and reflects the same approach set out in Article 15 of the International Covenant on Civil and Political Rights.

The Act combines two complementary approaches to incorporating international crimes into Canadian law. It refers to international law but also defines specific crimes at times. The three core crimes are defined by immediate reference to customary international law, conventional international law and general principles of law.

Canada's definition of genocide provides the specific *mens rea* set out in both the Genocide Convention and the Rome Statute, but does not describe any *actus reus*. Nor does it include the four types of group associations to which the Genocide Convention refers and, as a result, broadens the crime's scope to include "an identifiable group". For the *actus reus* aspect, a reference is made to international criminal law. As regards crimes against humanity, the Act follows the Rome Statute for the most part in describing the underlying crimes, while referring again to international law for the international or *chapeaux* elements. One notable exception is that the Act does not mention "enforced disappearances" and "apartheid". This was done because the legal status of these two crimes against humanity was considered uncertain under the Rome Statute and has not yet been tested for legality and, in particular, *vis-à-vis* the principle of non-retroactivity. The Act also expands the category of victims by not only using the notion of civilian population as in international criminal law but also by adding the concept of any identifiable group.

While the Act relies partially on the Rome Statute and international law to define genocide and crimes against humanity, it does not define war crimes at all. Rather, it refers to war crimes as a concept; it assumes that international law and practice will serve as the paramount source of judicial guidance regarding these crimes.

The Act has two interpretative provisions to clarify certain aspects of customary international law in relation to Canadian law. First, it explicitly indicates that the Rome Statute is its primary tool for all definitions in the Act by stating that,

> for greater certainty, crimes described in articles 6 and 7 and paragraph 2 of article 8 of the Rome Statute are, as of July 17, 1998, crimes according to customary international law, and may be crimes according to customary international law before that date. This does not limit or preju-

dice in any way the application of existing or developing rules of international law.

This enables the future jurisprudence to use the Rome Statute as a starting point for what constitutes customary international law, while at the same time allowing new developments in this area of international law to be taken into account. Secondly, it addressed an issue regarding customary international law raised by the Supreme Court of Canada in the *Finta* case. That court considered whether crimes against humanity existed during World War II and ruled that it was not convinced of their existence at the time. It did hold however that the terrible nature of the acts justified punishment in any event. In order to settle this issue, the Act states that crimes against humanity are were part of customary international law as of August 8, 1945, the date on which the International Military Tribunal was established in Nuremberg.

The Act is tightly and fundamentally connected to the Rome Statute. For that reason, the Act contains as appendices the text of the Statute's Articles 6, 7 and 8(2), to be used for direct reference.

D. Current cases

Rikhof referred to one on-going case in Canada in which the suspect was arrested in October 2005. The judge ruled that the suspect must remain in custody until the beginning of his trial in March 2007. This unusually lengthy pre-trial detention was ordered not on the basis of the danger that the suspect would pose to the community or because he would be a flight risk, but solely on the very serious nature of the war crimes for which he had been indicted, namely genocide, war crimes and crimes against humanity. This ruling exemplifies the Act's early impact.

E. Challenges

Rikhof noted that international criminal law has been and will continue to be in a state of flux. For instance, the elements of the crime against humanity of torture have changed over time. This would mean that, under the present Act in Canada, a prosecution against persons who might be charged for this crime committed in the 1970s will need to prove more elements than for the same crime committed more recently. Conceptually, this might not be easily acceptable to Canadian judges although a similar development with national crimes is not unusual. As well, judges may be reluctant to examine and use definitions developed for crimes in international criminal law which have their equivalent in Canadian law, such as murder or rape. They will be more naturally inclined to take domestic law as a point of departure and use the domestic definition of a crime rather than its international counterpart. For this latter aspect, another Supreme Court of Canada decision might provide some guidance in that it appears to favour an international approach over a national one. In the case of *Mugesera*, the court examined an immigration case, namely the deportation order against a permanent resident for the crime of hate speech committed in 1992. The speech was directed against Rwandan Tutsis and amounted to an incitement to commit genocide and murder, as well as the commission of the crime against humanity of murder and persecution. The court defined murder in a manner very similar to that found in the jurisprudence of the International Criminal Tribunal for the Former Yugoslavia (ICTY). Rulings such as this will give some confidence that courts may apply international definitions.

F. Conclusion

The Canadian approach has both advantages and disadvantages. Its advantage is that, by tying the regulation of core crimes very closely to international criminal law, it will be assured that Canada will never be out of step with new developments in the international sphere. By virtue of this link, these new developments automatically become part of Canadian law without the need of legislative amendments. The disadvantage is that this linkage requires all actors in criminal prosecutions to be continually up to date with changes in the international jurisprudence. As well, the exact relationship between domestic and international law is not certain at this point, including the status of domestic law where it has already gone beyond the requirements of international criminal law such as was done in defining the victims of genocide and crimes against humanity. The Act has not been tested in the courts yet, and these questions will no doubt be answered in the near future.

IV

The German Model[1]

A. Introduction

Claus Kreß, Professor, University of Cologne, noted that Germany ratified the Rome Statute on 11 December 2000 and its Bundestag and Bundesrat passed the Code of Crimes Under International Law (CCUIL) (*Völkerstrafgesetzbuch*) on 21 June 2002. The CCUIL, which entered into force on 26 June 2002, provides for universal jurisdiction over genocide, crimes against humanity and war crimes.[2]

B. Code of Crimes Against International Law

Kreß described the CCUIL as comprehensive, elaborate and maximalist. It contains three key elements. First, the CCUIL adopts a stand-alone approach in relation to Germany's existing criminal code. Second, it incorporates crimes under international law through autonomous translation. Third, it does not restrict its scope to the Rome Statute.

Germany decided against incorporating crimes under international law into its ordinary penal code. This decision was based on the difficulties in fitting special principles, such as those on superior orders and command responsibility, into one chapter of the general code. There was also a political rationale. By assembling core international crimes in a separate legal corpus, Germany would enhance their visibility and transmit an important and reassuring signal to the international community as regards the seriousness of these crimes.

1 This part of the minutes was prepared by Andreas M. Kravik.

2 Act Introducing the Code of Crimes Under International Law (*Gesetz zur Einführung des Völkerstrafgesetzbuchs*), BGBl.2002 I, P 2254 (Federal Law Gazette of the Federal Republic of Germany), 26 June 2002.

While based on the Rome Statute, the CCUIL defines crimes under international law via independent translation. It uses terminology familiar in German law, thereby improving accessibility to German jurists not used to dealing with international criminal standards. Autonomous translation enables German legislators to be more precise than the Rome Statute as regards the definitions of crimes. This approach would also allow for a more convincing structure than that contained in the Rome Statute's substantive law (cf., in particular, the different lists in Article 8).

The CCUIL incorporates not only offences enumerated in the Rome Statute but also those crimes as they are firmly grounded in general customary law. For example, for political reasons, the Rome Statute does not list the use of biological or chemical weapons as one of the core crimes. Yet, this crime under general customary international law is a war crime under Section 12 of the CCUIL.

C. Crimes under the CCUIL and the Rome Statute

Kreß went on to discuss the specific crimes — *i.e.*, genocide, crimes against humanity and war crimes — as they appear in the CCUIL and in the Rome Statute.

Genocide (CCUIL, Section 6). As regards genocide, Germany's intention has been to remain faithful to the text of the Rome Statute. This is mainly due to the text's long tradition. The Rome Statute reproduces word for word Article II of the Genocide Convention, a provision widely considered to reflect custom. There is one minor difference, however. The wording of the CCUIL allows for genocide to have occurred even if the conduct in question affects only one person (*e.g.* the killing of *a member* of a group; see CCUIL, Section 6(1)(1)). In contrast, the Rome Statute, on the face of it, envisages several persons being affected (*e.g.* the killing of *members* of the group; see Rome Statute, Article (6)(a)).[3]

[3] How the ICC will interpret this provision remains to be seen.

Crimes against humanity (CCUIL, Section 7). In the view of Kreß, this section of the CCUIL is less than perfect. Its imperfections, however, only mirror those of Article 7 of the Rome Statute. To begin with, some species of crimes against humanity are defined by reference to other rules of international law. For example, under Section 7(1)(4) of the CCUIL, it is a crime against humanity to deport or forcibly transfer "a person lawfully present in an area to another State or another area, in contravention of a *general rule of international law*". This formulation is problematic; the principle of specificity requires that criminal provisions be as detailed as possible and clearly indicate the conduct they prohibit. Nevertheless, German legislators found it impossible to attain greater precision than that found in Article 7 of the Rome Statute itself.

Another difficulty relates to the wording of Section 7(1)(7) of the CCUIL. This provision criminalises the causing of a person's enforced disappearance. Its problems emanate from the Elements of Crimes document adopted by the Assembly of States Parties. This offence establishes criminal liability as a result not only of a positive act (*litra a*) but also of an omission (*litra b*). Criminalising an omission implies the existence of an affirmative duty to act. And yet the precise source of law from which this affirmative duty stems remains unclear. Kreß suggested that the crime of enforced disappearance constitutes one instance in the process of incorporating crimes under international law into domestic criminal law where it would seem perfectly acceptable for national legislators first to wait for international case law to develop.

Article 7(1)(k) of the Rome Statute criminalises "other inhumane acts of a similar character intentionally causing great suffering, or serious injury to body or to mental or physical health". According to Kreß, Germany viewed this provision as an invitation to apply criminal prohibitions by analogy. Consequently, Section 8(1)(9) of the CCUIL limits the corresponding offence to threats against a person's physical integrity. Kreß considered this as a successful operation of enhancing legal certainty. Another success, in his opinion, is the CCUIL's treatment of the crime of apartheid as a special and aggravating instance of at least one other species of crimes against humanity.

War Crimes (CCUIL, Sections 8-12). War crimes can be committed in an international or internal armed conflict. Unlike the Rome Statute, the CCUIL eliminates this distinction as far as possible under customary international law and, to that extent, establishes one comprehensive list of crimes. This approach to the concept of war crimes has enabled Germany to maintain terminological consistency, a quality wanting in the Rome Statute. For example, Articles 8(2)(a)(i) and 8(2)(c)(i) of the Rome Statute use the expressions "wilful killing" and "murder", respectively, to refer to exactly the same act. Moreover, by abolishing the distinction between two separate lists of crimes according to the nature of the armed conflict, German judges need determine only whether one of the two criteria has been fulfilled. This is important, as in many cases the distinction between the two categories of armed conflict can be tenuous.

D. Concluding remarks

By way of conclusions, Kreß reflected on his experience in the drafting of the CCUIL. The drafting committee consisted of both criminal and public international lawyers. The two groups often presented different perspectives on the relationship between international and domestic law. This led to fruitful discussions and debates, a highly recommendable environment for endeavours of this nature.

V

Discussion on Particular Problems in Connection with the Import of Core International Crimes into National Criminal Law[1]

A. The role of the ICC Elements of Crimes document

The discussion opened with a short presentation by Joseph Rikhof on the ICC Elements of Crimes document. The document was developed by the Preparatory Committee following the adoption of the Rome Statute in 1998. While the ICC itself is not duty-bound to apply the elements of crimes as they are formulated in the document, it would be a useful means of interpretation. It would be especially relevant for those States which have provisions of international criminal law in their national legal systems.

One participant in the audience referred to her experience as a prosecutor in Denmark. Denmark has not engaged in any particular discussion on the import of core international criminal crimes into its domestic criminal law. International criminal law has simply not been imported into Danish law. Nor, as a prosecutor, had the participant missed it in her national legal system. She noted that those working directly with international crimes were not as well informed about the Elements of Crimes document as one would wish. As a result, the document was not much used.

In reply, Claus Kreß stressed that one would be ill-advised not to use the Elements of Crimes document when applying international criminal law. The document plays an important role in the codification of international crimes. One must be careful, however. A case in point is the formulation of the mental element in some crimes. For example, prosecuting war crimes against children involves proving intent con-

[1] This part of the minutes was prepared by Ingvild Dønnem Søyseth, Yassin Kaarshe and Andreas Kiaby.

cerning the victim's age. International criminal law defines the child as a person less than eighteen years of age. Defendants would often claim that they were unaware of the victim's age and therefore his or her status as a child. Should the prosecution fail to prove the defendants' knowledge in this regard, there would be no conviction. In order to overcome this hurdle, a "should have known" standard has been developed. This standard is different from the ICC Statute which requires intent.

According to another participant in the audience, the specific wording of the Rome Statute would not create serious problems as the crimes contained in the Statute are often very similar to those contained in national law. Murder, for instance, will mean the same in national law as in international criminal law. Problems arise when much is left to a judge's discretion.

Håkan Friman, Deputy Head of Division in the Ministry of Justice, Sweden, stated that Sweden plans to introduce a separate act on international crimes into its national law. The Elements of Crime document would be helpful when interpreting the Rome Statute. He was of the view that the use of the document in Nordic countries would provide inspirations for those seeking to clarify the content of international criminal law which has been imported into national law.

Stéphane J. Hankins argued that judges should take the Elements of the Crime document into account because it can serve as a guideline. The document should also be of significance to national legislators.

B. Modifying elements of crimes when importing core international crimes

Friman conceded that the elements of core international crimes have not yet been fully developed. Consequently, each State must assess the need of modifying these elements when importing them into its own legal system. There are considerations both in favour of and against modifying the elements of core international crimes. On the one hand, international criminal law becomes more precise through modification and this might prove necessary in order to satisfy the principle of legality in national systems. On the other hand, there will always be a risk of modified provisions departing from the international definitions and of weakening international law as a result.

One comment from the audience raised the prospects of all States modifying the elements of international crimes and, in so doing, adopting different approaches in their domestic law.

Kreß replied that changes might be technical only and ensuing problems might be solved through interpretation. Essentially, there are two approaches to importing international criminal law: one can either accept that there are differences or go back to the legislation and change the law.

Friman agreed that there are difficulties in bringing international and national law together. These difficulties become increasingly acute as international law, including the jurisprudence of international courts, continues to develop.

One member of the audience asked: What kind of international criminal law will one have if every State modifies it?

Kreß was of the opinion that international law might be modified in different ways. Regardless of the approach taken, however, one would always risk adopting provisions that differ from their original. How international criminal law will evolve in the future is a question of great importance, but unfortunately there are no easy answers to it.

Friman stated that introducing modified elements of crimes into domestic law is a political question that every State must consider. He proposed a list of "pros" and "cons" of elements modification. There are two items on the "pro" list:

- Modified crimes fit better within the general penal law and legal tradition of the State in question. This will make them more accessible to domestic courts and practitioners; and
- Modification may provide greater precision to the definition and hence greater compliance with the principle of legality as it is understood in the State concerned (there are differences among

different legal traditions as to what the principle of legality requires).

On Friman's contra list were:

- The risk that modified definitions would depart from the definitions in the Rome Statute;
- The risk that various modifications and their interpretations by the States concerned might contribute to the fragmentation of substantive law and the weakening of international law; and
- The risk that modifying definitions might mean failing the complementarity test (while the Rome Statute does not directly obligate States Parties to bring their substantive provisions in line with its own, such an obligation may well stem from other sources of international law).

Friman found it difficult to place some factors in the "pro" or "con" list. For example, there is a disparity among the ICTY jurisprudence, the ICTR jurisprudence and the Rome Statute in the definition of elements. In some respects, the Elements of Crimes document appears to depart from the explicit provisions of the Rome Statute; in other respects, the former does not read very well with the latter or, at least, leaves room for interpretation. Overcoming these uncertainties may promote and enhance the principle of legality. Redrafting problematic provisions may not always generate the desired outcome, however. It may very well result in references to different, but equally fluid, concepts.

Friman went on to state that it is in the interest of States to ensure that they are able to prosecute crimes to the same extent as the ICC would. It is so because they might consider certain cases very sensitive and, rather than to see the ICC intervene, wish to deal with these cases themselves under their own domestic law. However, the "complementarity" test gives States some leeway when deciding how to implement the crimes into domestic law: The Rome Statute contains provisions on admissibility and *non bis in idem* that are arguably more lenient for States than those in the ICTY and ICTR Statutes.

One attendee observed that, once the ICC began relying on the Elements of Crimes document and creating judicial practice, what had originally been considered optional might turn into something more binding. What would be the consequences of such a change for those States which had already modified the elements?

In the view of Kreß, the kind of changes Germany has made to the wording is more technical than substantial in nature. Germany's legislation obligates judges to interpret its provisions in conformity not only with international law but also with evolving international case law. The result would be that their rulings fully reflect international case law and comport with the principle of legality, *i.e.*, to the extent allowed by the specific wording adopted in German law.

Nevertheless, Kreß agreed that there are discrepancies which cannot be resolved through interpretation alone. It may well be that international case law develops in such a way that it can no longer be captured within the specific meaning that the law of a State ascribes to a given definition. National legislatures which do not adopt a global approach to this matter have two political options. One option would be that they accept the discrepancies and decline to convict a person who would otherwise be convicted under the more lenient international standards. The other would be that they turn to their legislatures and inform them that international case law has evolved and that their national text needs to be revised accordingly.

C. War crimes not included in the ICC Statute

Mads Harlem, Legal Adviser for the Norwegian Red Cross, presented what in his view constituted an overview, rather than a complete catalogue, of crimes not included in the ICC Statute. It was not his intention to offer any conclusion as to whether these crimes should or should not be adopted into national legislation.[2]

[2] Harlem has prepared a supplementary article entitled "Importing War Crimes into Norwegian Legislation" in which he discusses the situation in Norway. The article is included in this publication; see below.

Harlem listed the following as examples of crimes not included in the ICC Statute:

- Launching an attack against works or installations containing dangerous forces in the knowledge that such an attack will cause excessive loss of civilian life, injury to civilians, damage to civilian objects, or a combination thereof, as defined in Article 57(2)(a)(iii), Additional Protocol I (when committed wilfully, in violation of the relevant provisions of the Protocol, and causing death or serious injury to body or health);
- Unjustifiable delay in the repatriation of prisoners of war;
- Acts listed under Article 8(2)(a) of the ICC Statute when committed against persons protected by Additional Protocol I but not the Geneva Conventions;
- Serious violations of Additional Protocol II to the 1954 Hague Convention for the Protection of Cultural Property (they only partially overlap Article 8 of the ICC Statute);
- Grave breaches of Additional Protocol I when committed against: (a) persons in the power of an adverse party who are protected by Articles 44, 45 and 73 of the Protocol; (b) the wounded, sick and shipwrecked of the adverse party who are protected by the Protocol; and (c) those medical or religious personnel, medical units or medical transports which are under the control of the adverse party and are protected by the Protocol;
- Use of certain weapons, including: (a) binding lasers, prohibited by Protocol IV to the Certain Conventional Weapons Convention; (b) anti-personnel landmines, prohibited by the Convention on the Prohibition of the Use, Stockpiling, Production and Transfer of Anti-Personnel Mines and on their Destruction; and (c) others, e.g., cluster munitions, as may be prohibited in some States (if they are prohibited in some States, should they also be prohibited under the ICC Statute?);
- Compulsory recruitment of persons between fifteen and eighteen years of age (States Parties to the Convention on the Rights of the Child are duty-bound to ensure that persons who have not at-

tained the age of fifteen years are not compulsorily recruited into their armed forces; the ICC Statute designates breaches of this obligation as a war crime; the Optional Protocol to the Convention raises the relevant age to eighteen years; should those States which are party both to the Optional Protocol and to the ICC Statute raise the age to eighteen years?);

- War crimes committed in a non-international armed conflict falling below the threshold of Articles 1 and 2 of Additional Protocol II yet to which common Article 3 applies (Article 8(2)(d) and (f) of the ICC Statute refers to the more restrictive criteria applicable to Additional Protocol II; should the Statute be amended to refer to the broader criteria applicable to common Article 3?); and
- Misuse of the new emblem protected by Additional Protocol III.

One participant in the audience observed that a basic element had been missing in the discussion so far. An impression has been created that one may decide for oneself, as if from an *a la carte* menu, which crimes should be adopted in the national legislation. Yet there is a big difference between the German model of elaborating on genocide as a crime, on the one hand, and the Canadian model of taking out enforced disappearances, on the other hand. Additions and elaborations are to be welcome, but States ought to be loyal to their commitments. One should proceed with great caution when implementing the ICC obligations and be very careful when taking elements out of the legal catalogue.

Rikhof agreed that taking things out of the legal catalogue could be problematic. However, when, as in the Canadian model, the specific offences in the list of crimes in the Rome Statute are not completely implemented while at the same time there is a general reference to customary international law, it is likely that the entire body of core offences of that Statute is presumed to be part of the domestic legislation. Referring to customary law in effect creates more flexibility in the sense that the crimes in national legislation develop in parallel with customary international law. With respect to the specific crimes against humanity of "enforced disappearance" and "apartheid", there is certainly a strong argument that these crimes are not new. The crime of "enforced disappearance" was mentioned in the Nuremberg judgement under the discussion regarding the "Nacht und Nebel order"; the crime of "apartheid" can be found in the 1973 International Convention on the Suppression and Punishment of the Crime of Apartheid. Rikhof recommended the *Tadić*-approach to dealing with customary law and national legislation. The four *Tadić* criteria for defining customary law make it possible to discern new crimes which are not stated in the Rome Statute. It is not a bad thing to add or clarify new crimes. If several States elaborate and further define core crimes, such elaborations and definitions may give rise to emerging customary law.

D. Conclusion[3]

Tørris Jæger, Head of the International Humanitarian Law Unit of the Norwegian Red Cross, reiterated the purpose of the seminar. The purpose was not only to discuss how to import core international crimes into national criminal law, but also to put the matter on Norway's political agenda.

Jæger recalled that Hankins' presentation outlined the various means of importation and considered different options. The Canadian model, as described by Rikhof, revealed the difficulties and importance of finding solutions and appropriate ways to draft legislation so that it becomes applicable, understood and relevant within the national context. Kreß's explanation of the maximalist approach in Germany highlighted its stand-alone solution and autonomous translation, as well as its scope going beyond treaty rules to encompass customary international law. The plenary discussion which followed these presentations explored the different possibilities, challenges and opportunities that lay ahead. Particular attention was given to the possibility of divergences between the way in which national and international law may develop.

Jæger noted that Canada is currently dealing with cases going back to the 1940's up to the 1990's. It is incumbent upon the Norwe-

[3] This part of the minutes was prepared by Ellen Stensrud.

gian government to accept the intellectual challenge to which Kreß referred. Jæger expressed his hope that Norway would adopt as maximalist and dynamic as possible an approach when importing core international crimes.

6

Importing War Crimes into Norwegian Legislation

Mads Harlem*

1. Introduction

Importing genocide, crimes against humanity and war crimes into national criminal law is significant for several reasons, including those found in treaty law as well as in the law and practice of international criminal jurisdictions. The Rome Statute of the International Criminal Court (ICC) provides in its preamble that "it is the duty of every State to exercise its criminal jurisdiction over those responsible for international crimes". States are also obligated under treaties such as the Genocide Convention, the Geneva Conventions and the Torture Convention to enact legislation which gives effect to their prohibitions within national criminal law. The Appeals Chamber of the International Criminal Tribunal for Rwanda (ICTR) decided in *Bagaragaza* that it "cannot sanction the referral of a case to a jurisdiction for trial where the conduct cannot be charged as a serious violation of international humanitarian law".[1] This shows the importance the ICTR attaches to the notion that national jurisdiction characterise the conduct in question as genocide, crimes against humanity and war crimes rather than as ordinary crimes.

Many States have already imported core international crimes into national criminal law.[2] This is in accordance with the spirit of the

* Legal Adviser, Norwegian Red Cross. The article reflects the views of the author alone and not necessarily those of the Norwegian Red Cross.

1 *Prosecutor v. Michel Bagaragaza*, Case No. ICTR-05-86-AR11*bis*, *Decision on Rule 11*bis *Appeal*, 30 August 2006, para. 18.

2 See, *e.g.*, Canada's Crimes Against Humanity and War Crimes Act of 2000, c. 24, and Germany's Act to Introduce the Code of Crimes Under International Law (*Völkerstrafgesetzbuch*) of 26 June 2002.

ICC's complementarity principle according to which the Court should be seized of a case only in the event that national criminal justice systems are "unable or unwilling" to genuinely investigate and prosecute it.[3] Conversely, if a national court is "able and willing" to prosecute a case, that court shall take priority over the ICC.

In 2004, Norway's Penal Code Commission proposed that separate provisions on genocide, crimes against humanity and war crimes be inserted into Norwegian criminal law. At a public consultation held in April 2007, the Ministry of Justice made a proposal on such provisions.[4] The proposal is expected to be presented to Parliament in the autumn of 2007.

That the process of incorporation has finally begun in Norway is encouraging. It is important to keep in mind, however, that Norway's international law commitments go beyond the crimes covered in the Rome Statute. This paper identifies war crimes which have not been included in the ICC Statute, but still should become part of Norwegian criminal law. It will also be argued that Norway should not limit its definition of war crimes to those defined as such under international law; rather, it should include acts committed in an armed conflict which violate values of warfare that are important to Norway.

2. War crimes as a notion

The distinction between lawful and unlawful acts of war is central when defining war crimes. Combatants are immune from prosecution in respect of lawful acts of war, *e.g.*, killing an able-bodied, non-surrendering enemy combatant without resource to unlawful means and methods of warfare. They remain so even where the same acts

[3] See Article 17, ICC Statute. As noted earlier, the ICTR denied a motion to refer the *Bagaragaza* case to Norway for trial. It did so on the ground that Norway would treat the crimes charged as ordinary crimes rather than serious violations of international humanitarian law. The ICC might one day take a similar view and hold that ordinary crimes do not satisfy the "ability" requirement under Article 17 of the ICC Statute.

[4] This article does not deal with the content of this proposal.

otherwise constitute ordinary crimes, *e.g.*, murder.[5] They are not immune from prosecution, however, in respect of acts in breach of the laws and customs of war. In general, if such acts are regarded as serious, they are defined as war crimes in international criminal law.

However, there is no generally accepted definition of "war crimes" in international law. Rule 156 of the customary international humanitarian law study prepared by the International Committee of the Red Cross (hereinafter, "*Customary Law Study*")[6] defines war crimes as "serious violations of international humanitarian law".[7] The four Geneva Conventions of 1949 and their Additional Protocol I of 1977 specify violations of certain provisions as their "grave breaches"; Additional Protocol I, in turn, designates such "grave breaches" as "war crimes".

In *Tadić*, the International Criminal Tribunal for the Former Yugoslavia (ICTY) rendered an interlocutory appeal decision (hereinafter, "*Tadić* Jurisdiction Decision")[8] in which it stated that:

i. A war crime must constitute an infringement of a rule of international humanitarian law;
ii. The rule must be customary in nature, or covered by treaty law which is unquestionably binding on the parties at the time of the alleged offence and not in conflict with or derogating from per-

---

[5] Other persons who participate directly in hostilities do not enjoy immunity from prosecution in respect of those acts arising from their participation which constitute ordinary crimes.

[6] Jean-Marie Henckaerts and Louise Doswald-Beck, *Customary International Humanitarian Law* (Cambridge University Press, 2005). This publication is the result of a major international study of current State practice with a view to identifying the content of customary international humanitarian law. Presented in two volumes, it analyses the customary rules of international humanitarian law and contains a detailed summary of the relevant treaty law and State practice throughout the world.

[7] Rule 156, *Customary Law Study*.

[8] See *Prosecutor v. Duško Tadić a/k/a "Dule"*, Case No. IT-94-1-AR72, *Decision on the Defence Motion for Interlocutory Appeal on Jurisdiction*, 2 October 1995 ("*Tadić* Jurisdiction Decision").

emptory norms of international law including most customary rules of international humanitarian law;

iii. The violation must be "serious", that is to say, it must constitute a breach of a rule protecting important values, and the breach must involve grave consequences for the victim; and

iv. The violation of the rule must entail, under customary or conventional law, the individual criminal responsibility of the person breaching the rule.[9]

In the same decision, the ICTY gave the following as an example of non-serious violations:

> [T]he fact of a combatant simply appropriating a loaf of bread in an occupied village would not amount to a "serious violation of international humanitarian law" although it may be regarded as falling foul of the basic principle laid down in Article 46, paragraph 1, of the Hague Regulations (and the corresponding rule of customary international law) whereby "private property must be respected" by any army occupying an enemy territory.[10]

The State practice as laid down in the *Tadić* Jurisdiction Decision and in the *Customary Law Study* indicates that the expression "war crimes" means serious violations of international humanitarian law. It does not exclude the possibility however that a State may define other violations of the laws or customs of war as war crimes as well. Caution is in order when including crimes which are not linked to an armed conflict, lest their inclusion create discrepancies between penal provisions in national and international law. Nevertheless, States should not hesitate to criminalise acts that are linked to an armed conflict and breach important values in warfare.

The list of war crimes enumerated in Article 8 of the ICC Statute is the result of complicated international negotiations. Many acts otherwise regarded as war crimes under treaty law and/or customary law were left out in order to reach the broadest consensus possible. Ac-

---

9 See *Tadić* Jurisdiction Decision, paras. 94 and 143.

10 *Tadić* Jurisdiction Decision, para. 94.

cordingly, Article 8 does not include all serious violations of international humanitarian law. This should not keep Norway from criminalising these and other violations of international law. On the contrary, in accordance with the *Tadić* Jurisdiction Decision and customary law, Norway's war crimes provisions should include:

i. Serious violations of treaty provisions binding upon Norway in armed conflict;
ii. Serious violations of customary law applicable in armed conflict; and
iii. Violations of law which are not regarded as serious but still linked to an armed conflict and in breach of important values of warfare.

3. War crimes not included in the ICC Statute

3.1. Preliminary remarks

The war crimes listed below are to a large extent based on the four Geneva Conventions of 1949, their Additional Protocols I and II of 1977 and Rule 156 of the *Customary Law Study*.[11]

In order for given conduct to amount to a war crime, it must have a link to an armed conflict. International humanitarian law has traditionally distinguished between international armed conflicts including situations of military occupation, on the one hand, and non-international armed conflicts, on the other hand. An international armed conflict is defined as fighting between the armed forces of at least two States. The Geneva Conventions, Additional Protocol I and customary international humanitarian law apply to such a conflict. A non-international armed conflict is defined as fighting on the territory

[11] Rule 156 of the *Customary Law Study* states: "Serious violations of international law constitute war crimes". For crimes not mentioned in Rule 156 but regarded as serious violations of international humanitarian law and elaborated in the summary of that rule, see *Customary Law Study*, Volume I: Rules, pp. 568-603. Reference will also be made below to several other international humanitarian law treaties, including Protocol II of 1999 to the 1954 Hague Cultural Property Convention and various weapons conventions.

of a State between the regular armed forces and identifiable armed groups, or between such groups. Rules applicable to non-international armed conflicts include Article 3 common to the four Geneva Conventions, Additional Protocol II and a growing body of customary international humanitarian law.[12]

The Geneva Conventions and Additional Protocol I designate specific acts as their "grave breaches" and explicitly obligate the High Contracting Parties to repress them criminally.[13] These breaches will be elaborated below.

Unlike the Geneva Conventions and Additional Protocol I, neither common Article 3 nor Additional Protocol II contains any express obligation to repress their breaches. In recent years, however, it has become increasingly common for a given treaty both to apply the same body of rules to international and non-international armed conflicts and to provide for sanctions in the event of their serious violations.[14] Also, customary law has clearly affirmed an obligation for States to repress serious violations of international humanitarian law committed in non-international armed conflicts. Even though this customary obligation may not extend to all violations, Norway should still define as war crimes serious violations committed in both international and non-international armed conflicts alike. As will be argued in Section 4, Norway should as far as possible eliminate the distinction between international and non-international armed conflicts in its war crimes provisions.

International case-law indicates that the mental state generally required for war crimes is wilfulness, *i.e.*, either intention or reckless-

[12] Additional Protocol II of 1977 has a more restrictive scope of application than that of Article 3 common to the four Geneva Conventions. See below, under Section 3.2.2.

[13] See Article 49, Geneva Convention I; Article 50, Geneva Convention II; Article 129, Geneva Convention III; Article 146, Geneva Convention IV; and Article 85, Additional Protocol I.

[14] See, *e.g.*, Protocol II on Prohibitions or Restrictions on the Use of Mines, Booby-Traps and Other Devices as amended on 3 May 1996 annexed to the Certain Conventional Weapons Convention of 1980.

ness. The precise mental element varies from war crime to war crime, however. This article does not consider the matter further.

3.2. List of war crimes not included in the ICC Statute

3.2.1. Threshold for the application of war crimes enumerated in Article 8(1)

Article 8(1) provides that the ICC shall have jurisdiction in respect of war crimes "in particular when committed as part of plan or policy or as part of a large-scale commission of such crimes". This is a threshold for the Court's jurisdiction rather than an additional element of the crimes listed in Article 8. This threshold is intended to prevent the ICC from being overburdened with minor or isolated cases. The expression "in particular" indicates that the ICC does retain jurisdiction over war crimes *not* committed "as part of a plan or policy or as part of a large-scale commission of such crimes". Hence, there is no reason for this threshold to be included in the Norwegian provisions on war crimes.

3.2.2. The term "non-international armed conflict" in the ICC Statute

Article 8(2)(c) of the ICC Statute is based on common Article 3. Common Article 3 regulates non-international armed conflicts and is considered customary. The threshold for the application of common Article 3 is very low. One would expect that Article 8(2)(c) has a similarly low threshold of application.

According to Article 8(2)(d) of the ICC Statute, however, Article 8(2)(c) "does not apply to situations of internal disturbances and tensions, such as riots, isolated and sporadic acts of violence or other acts of a similar nature". This language is taken from Article 1(2) of Additional Protocol II, an instrument which otherwise "develops and supplements [common Article 3] without modifying its existing conditions of application".[15] In other words, Article 8(2)(d) of the ICC Statute effectively raises the application threshold of Article 8(2)(c), which

[15] Article 1(1), Additional Protocol II.

criminalises violations of the rules contained in common Article 3, to that of Additional Protocol II. This higher threshold should be removed in Norwegian legislation.

Nor should Article 8(3) of the ICC Statute be incorporated into Norwegian law. This provision was inserted as a result of the pressure from a number of States opposed to the inclusion of war crimes committed during internal armed conflicts.

3.2.3. Protected persons and Property under Article 8(2)(a) of the ICC Statute

Article 8(2)(a) covers certain offences committed against persons or property protected under the relevant Geneva Conventions. Within the meaning of Geneva Conventions I and II, protected persons and objects are the sick, wounded and shipwrecked, as well as medical personnel and equipment. Geneva Conventions III and IV protect prisoners of war (POWs) and certain categories of civilian persons,[16] respectively.

Additional Protocol I enlarges the groups of persons and property protected in international armed conflict to include:

i. Persons who have taken part in hostilities and have fallen into the power of an adverse Party within the meaning of Articles 44 (combatants and POWs) and 45 (protection of persons who have taken part in hostilities) of Additional Protocol I. This definition is broader than that of POWs in Geneva Convention III.
ii. Refugees and stateless persons within the meaning of Article 73 of Additional Protocol I. Article 75 entitles them to protection under Geneva Convention IV.
iii. The wounded, sick and shipwrecked of the adverse Party. Article 8(a) and (b) of Additional Protocol I enlarges the corresponding categories as defined in Geneva Conventions I and II.

[16] Geneva Convention IV protects civilians who are not entitled to POW status and, at any given moment and in any manner whatsoever, find themselves, in the case of a conflict or occupation, in the hands of a Party to the conflict or Occupying Power of which they are not nationals. See Article 4, Geneva Convention IV.

iv. Medical or religious personnel, medical units and transports under the control of the adverse Party. Article 8(c), (d), (e) and (g) of Additional Protocol I broadens the protection of these groups of persons and property compared to the Geneva Conventions. The expression "under the control of the adverse Party" is justified by the fact that such persons and objects may come from a non-belligerent State, an aid society recognised and authorised by such a State or even an impartial international humanitarian organisation.

Article 8(2)(a) of the ICC Statute contains grave breaches of the Geneva Conventions but not grave breaches of Additional Protocol I. This is so because Additional Protocol I has not as a whole enjoyed the same universal acceptance as the Geneva Conventions. However, Norway is a party to the Protocol. Thus, there is no reason why Norway should not criminalise conduct mentioned in Article 8(2)(a) of the ICC Statute when it is committed against persons or objects protected under Additional Protocol I.

3.2.4. Violations of international humanitarian law not included in the list of war crimes under Article 8(2)(b) and (e) of the ICC Statute

3.2.4.1. Intentionally launching an attack in the knowledge that such attack will cause incidental loss of life or injury to civilians or damage to civilian objects or widespread, long-term and severe to the natural environment which would be clearly excessive in relation to the concrete and direct overall military advantage anticipated

When such an attack is launched during an international armed conflict, it constitutes a war crime under Article 8(2)(b)(iv) of the ICC Statute. The word "overall" is neither contained in Articles 51 and 85 of Additional Protocol I, nor found in the corresponding rules of customary international law as they have been identified in Rule 14 of the Customary Law Study. According to the same study, the word "overall" does not add an extra element[17]; it could therefore be kept in Norway's war crimes provisions.

Additional Protocol II does not explicitly refer to the principle of proportionality. Rule 14 of the *Customary Law Study* states however that it is a customary rule applicable in non-international armed conflicts.

The ICC Statute does not list an intentional violation of this principle committed in non-international armed conflicts as a war crime. Nor is it, as such, defined as a grave breach in any treaty provisions or considered a serious violation of customary law. However, Article 14(2) of Amended Protocol II to the 1980 Convention on Certain Conventional Weapons obligates its States parties, including Norway, to punish persons who wilfully kill civilians or cause serious injury to them. Article 3(8)(c) of the same Protocol espouses the principle of proportionality in attacks. Launching attacks in breach of the principle in a non-international armed conflict appears as a war crime in Section 11(1)(3) of Germany's Act to Introduce the Code of Crimes Under International Law. Since the said conduct in a non-international armed conflict is inconsistent with important values of warfare, Norway should also treat it as a war crime.

3.2.4.2. Making a person the object of attack in the knowledge that he is hors de combat

Article 8(2)(b)(vi) of the ICC Statute criminalises only the killing or wounding of combatants who have surrendered at discretion. By virtue of Article 85(3)(e) of Additional Protocol I, however, making a person the object of attack in the knowledge that he is *hors de combat* constitutes a grave breach of that Protocol. The *Customary Law Study* also identifies it as a war crime.[18] Norway should follow the approach taken in this study.

The same conduct committed in a non-international armed conflict is covered in Article 8(2)(c) of the ICC Statute.

---

[17] See *Customary Law Study*, Volume I: Rules, p. 577.

[18] See *Customary Law Study*, Volume I: Rules, pp. 575-576.

3.2.4.3. Making medical or religious personnel, medical units or medical transports the object of attack

Under the ICC Statute, this act constitutes a war crime only if the personnel, units or objects concerned use the distinctive emblems of the Geneva Conventions.[19] Additional Protocol I treats such conduct as its grave breach, however, regardless of the use of the said emblems. Medical or religious personnel are also protected under Articles 9 and 11 of Additional Protocol II. The *Customary Law Study* identifies making medical or religious personnel, medical units or medical transports the object of attack as a war crime in both international and non-international armed conflict.[20]

Other than the ICC Statute, no relevant treaty provision binding on Norway refers to the use of the distinctive emblems of the Geneva Conventions as an element of this offence. It should therefore not be kept in Norway's war crimes provisions.

3.2.4.4. Pillage or other taking of property contrary to international humanitarian law

Under Article 8(2)(b)(xvi) and (e)(v) of the ICC Statute, only "pillaging a town or place, even when taken by assault", is regarded as a war crime. In contrast, Article 33, second paragraph, of Geneva Convention IV prohibits pillage *as such* in international armed conflict; so does Article 4(2) of Additional Protocol II in non-international armed conflict. Even though pillage or other taking of property contrary to international humanitarian law does not constitute a grave breach of any treaty, it does, according to the *Customary Law Study*, constitute a war crime in both international and non-international armed conflict.[21] Norway should import this war crime into its legislation.

---

[19] See Article 8(2)(b)(xxiv) and (e)(ii), ICC Statute.

[20] See *Customary Law Study*, Volume I: Rules, pp. 575-576 and 593-597.

[21] See *Customary Law Study*, Volume I: Rules, pp. 575-576 and 591-593.

3.2.4.5. Unjustifiable delay in the repatriation of POWs or civilians

This war crime is not mentioned in the ICC Statute but should nevertheless be imported into Norwegian legislation. Article 85(4)(b) of Additional Protocol I describes unjustifiable delay in the repatriation of POWs or civilians as a grave breach of the Protocol; the *Customary Law Study* identifies it as a war crime if committed in an international armed conflict.[22]

Under both customary law and treaty law, this war crime only applies to international armed conflicts. This is so because the POW status only exists in international armed conflicts. According to Rule 128(c) of the *Customary Law Study*, however, persons deprived of their liberty in relation to a non-international armed conflict must be released as soon as the reasons for the deprivation of their liberty cease to exist. Even though customary law does not regard violations of this rule as a war crime, Norway should still do so in its national legislation since they violate values of warfare that are important to Norway.

3.2.4.6. Making improper use of a flag of truce, of the flag or the military insignia and uniform of the enemy or of the United Nations, as well as of the distinctive emblems of the Geneva Conventions, resulting in death or serious personal injury

This is regarded as a war crime in Article 8(2)(b)(vii) of the ICC Statute. According to Article 85(3)(f) of Additional Protocol I, the perfidious use of the distinctive emblem of the Red Cross, Red Crescent or Red Lion and Sun or other protective signs recognised by the Geneva Conventions or the Protocol, constitutes a grave breach of that Protocol.

The ICC Statute does not criminalise this conduct in non-international armed conflicts; nor does the *Customary Law Study* identify it as a war crime in such conflicts. Insofar as the underlying prohibition protects important values of warfare, however, Norway should

---

[22] See *Customary Law Study*, Volume I: Rules, pp. 586-588.

still treat violations of this prohibition as a war crime if committed in a non-international armed conflict.

In the ICC Statute, only the improper use of the Geneva Convention emblems is regarded as a war crime. This means that making improper use of the new emblem adopted in Additional Protocol III of 2005 falls outside the scope of the ICC Statute. According to the Protocol's Article 6(1), however, those provisions of the Geneva Conventions and, where applicable, Additional Protocols I and II, which govern the prevention and repression of misuse of the distinctive emblems, shall apply equally to the Additional Protocol III emblem. Even though this rule is not customary, Norway is still a party to Additional Protocol III. The war crimes provisions in Norway should therefore also cover both the new and existing emblems or signs designed to protect people or objects in armed conflict.

3.2.4.7. Using starvations of civilians as a method of warfare by depriving them of objects indispensable to their survival, including wilfully impeding relief supplies

Under Article 8(2)(b)(xxv) of the ICC Statute, this is regarded as a war crime only in an international armed conflict.

Even in non-international armed conflicts, however, using starvation of civilians as a method of warfare by depriving them of objects indispensable to their survival, including wilfully impeding relief supplies, is in breach of Articles 14 and 18 of Additional Protocol II and identified as a war crime in the *Customary Law Study*.[23] Thus, it should be imported into Norway's war crimes provisions for both international and non-international armed conflicts.

3.2.4.8. Making non-defended localities and demilitarised zones the object of attack

Attacking such localities and zones is not mentioned as a war crime in the ICC Statute but appears in Article 85(3)(d) of Additional Protocol I as its grave breach. According to the *Customary Law Study*, the act

[23] See *Customary Law Study*, Volume I: Rules, pp. 599-603.

constitutes a war crime in both international and non-international armed conflict.[24] This should be included in the Norwegian war crimes legislation.

3.2.4.9. Slavery and deportation to slave labour

Neither slavery nor deportation to slave labour is mentioned in Article 8 of the ICC Statute. The *Customary Law Study*, however, identifies such practice as a war crime in both international and non-international armed conflict.[25] The crime should therefore be imported into Norwegian legislation.

3.2.4.10. Collective punishment

The ICC Statute does not mention this crime. Collective punishment is prohibited, however, under Geneva Conventions III and IV as well as Article 4(2)(b) of Additional Protocol II. It is also identified as a war crime in the *Customary Law Study*.[26] Norway should therefore incorporate this crime for both international and non-international armed conflicts.

3.2.4.11. Despoliation of the wounded, sick, shipwrecked or dead

Despoliation of the wounded, sick, shipwrecked or dead is not mentioned in the ICC Statute but should be part of Norway's war crimes provisions. Whether in an international or non-international armed conflict, States are obligated to take all possible measures to protect the wounded, sick and shipwrecked from pillage and ill-treatment.[27] Whereas none of the Geneva Conventions, nor Additional Protocol I, describes despoliation of the wounded, sick, shipwrecked or dead as a grave breach, it is regarded as a war crime under customary law in an

---

[24] See *Customary Law Study*, Volume I: Rules, pp. 576-578 and 599-603.

[25] See *Customary Law Study*, Volume I: Rules, pp. 586 and 599-602.

[26] See *Customary Law Study*, Volume I: Rules, pp. 586-587 and 599-603.

[27] See Article 15, first paragraph, Geneva Convention I; Article 8, Additional Protocol II.

international armed conflict.[28] The *Customary Law Study* does not identify this as a war crime in a non-international armed conflict. Norway should still treat it as such in both international and non-international armed conflicts because it is contrary to important values of warfare.

3.2.4.12. Attacking or ill-treating a parlementaire or bearer of the flag of truce

This conduct is not criminalised under the ICC Statute. Nevertheless, it is a violation of the Hague Regulations and of customary international law.[29] Norway should treat it as a war crime in both international and non-international armed conflicts.

3.2.4.13. Launching an attack against works or installations containing dangerous forces in the knowledge that such attack will cause excessive loss of life, injury to civilians or damage to civilian objects

The ICC Statute does not enumerate this crime. It does appear, however, as a grave breach in Article 85(3)(c) of Additional Protocol I and as a customary war crime in the Customary Law Study.[30] Article 15 of Additional Protocol II prohibits attacks against works or installations containing dangerous forces. Norwegian legislation should designate this conduct as a war crime in both international and non-international armed conflict since it breaches important values of warfare.

3.2.4.14. Using human shields

Article 8(2)(b)(xxiii) of the ICC Statute criminalises the use of human shields in an international armed conflict. The Statutes contains no comparable provisions for non-international armed conflict, however. Norway's war crimes provisions should still corporate it for non-

[28] See *Customary Law Study*, Volume I: Rules, pp. 586-588.

[29] See *Customary Law Study*, Volume I: Rules, p. 586.

[30] See *Customary Law Study*, Volume I: Rules, pp. 586-590.

international armed conflict, in accordance with the findings of the *Customary Law Study*.[31]

3.2.4.15. Making civilian objects the object of attack

This constitutes a war crime under the ICC Statute only if committed during an international armed conflict. The *Customary Law Study*, however, identifies it as a war crime also in a non-international armed conflict.[32] Norway should follow the approach taken by the *Customary Law Study* on this offence.

3.2.4.16. Use of prohibited weapons

The ICC Statute criminalises the use of weapons only if they are prohibited under customary law. The Statute does not criminalise the use of any specific weapons during a non-international armed conflict.

Norway should treat as a war crime not only the use of weapons banned under customary international law but also the use of weapons banned by conventions to which it has acceded. Section 107 of Norway's Military Penal Code applies to the latter but not the former. A provision should be included in Norwegian legislation on war crimes so that the ban has a general application. The following wording could rectify the situation:

> Use of weapons, projectiles and equipment and methods of warfare which have been banned in accordance with Norway's international legal obligations.

3.2.4.17. Serious violations of Protocol II to the 1954 Hague Cultural Property Convention

The ICC Statute does not cover all of the acts punishable under Protocol II to the 1954 Hague Convention. Examples include theft, pillage or misappropriation of, or acts of vandalism directed against, cultural property protected under the Protocol in both international and non-

[31] See *Customary Law Study*, Volume I: Rules, pp. 599-602.

[32] See *Customary Law Study*, Volume I: Rules, pp. 597-598.

international armed conflict. Such acts should be included in the Norwegian provision on war crimes.

3.2.4.18. Child soldiers

Conscripting or enlisting children under fifteen into national armed forces, or using them to participate actively in hostilities, constitutes a war crime under Article 8(2)(b)(xxvi) of the ICC Statute. This was an extremely controversial topic during the negotiations, and the age adopted was based on the minimum standards contained in Article 77(2) and (3) of Additional Protocol I.[33]

Norway is party to Additional Protocol II to the Convention on the Rights of the Child which defines child soldiers as those under eighteen. Norway's war crimes provisions should follow this definition.

4. Methods of incorporating war crimes into Norwegian legislation

War crimes can be committed in both international and non-international armed conflicts. The substantive definitions of these crimes are more or less the same. Unlike the ICC Statute, Norwegian legislation should eliminate the distinction between war crimes committed in international armed conflict and those committed in non-international armed conflict.

There are various ways in which war crimes might be incorporated into Norwegian penal legislation. This could be done through the adoption of generic provisions or specific provisions enumerating all conduct mentioned in Section 3 above and in the ICC Statute.

Adopting generic provisions is simple. No new national legislation will be needed when existing treaties are amended, when Norway becomes a party to a new treaty or when new customary law has been identified. Generic provisions would absorb new treaties to which Norway could become a party and new customary law which could

[33] See the bill before the Norwegian Parliament (St. prp. no. 24 (1999-2000)), p. 86.

become binding on it in the future. For the reasons discussed earlier, this approach is particularly suitable for criminalising the use of prohibited weapons. It could also be used for several of the other crimes listed above.

At the same time, however, generic provisions may prove problematic *vis-à-vis* the principle of legality. Norway would ensure greater respect for this principle by specifying the entire list of offences in its war crimes provisions. One major setback of specific criminalisation is that it requires considerable research and drafting; this would be a major task for the legislator. Furthermore, excessive detail and specificity might deprive Norway of the flexibility needed to incorporate relevant developments in international law at a later stage.

A mixed approach would probably be more effective when importing war crimes into Norwegian legislation. Such an approach involves criminalisation through generic provisions combined with the explicit and specific criminalisation of certain serious offences. This combination permits Norway to carry out all its treaty obligations concerning the repression of breaches of international humanitarian law without undermining its respect for the principle of legality.

5. Conclusion

Norway ratified the ICC Statute on 16 February 2000. The Statute establishes a permanent International Criminal Court vested with the authority to institute criminal proceedings against and judge individuals for genocide, crimes against humanity and war crimes.

As argued in this article, States should enact separate penal provisions for these crimes in their national legislation. It is not sufficient to penalise such offences in accordance with ordinary criminal provisions relating to rape, coercion, threats, the deprivation of liberty, murder, and the like.

The ICC was established as a result of complicated international negotiations. States should not hesitate to include offences other than those mentioned in the relevant crime categories of the ICC Statues.

It appears that the war crimes provisions proposed by the Norwegian Ministry of Justice correspond to the ICC Statute in their definition of war crimes. Moreover, they criminalise other serious violations of the laws and customs of war as well. It is hoped that Norway will soon fully comply with all its international obligations elaborated in this article.

FICHL PUBLICATION SERIES

OTHER VOLUMES IN THE FICHL PUBLICATION SERIES

Nobuo Hayashi (editor):
National Military Manuals on the Law of Armed Conflict
Torkel Opsahl Academic EPublisher
Oslo, 2010
FICHL Publication Series No. 2 (Second Edition, 2010)
ISBN 978-82-93081-02-9
The Second Edition was published 23 July 2010
The First Edition was published 19 December 2008.

Morten Bergsmo, Kjetil Helvig, Ilia Utmelidze and Gorana Žagovec:
The Backlog of Core International Crimes Case Files in Bosnia and Herzegovina
Torkel Opsahl Academic EPublisher
Oslo, 2010
FICHL Publication Series No. 3 (Second Edition, 2010)
ISBN 978-82-93081-04-3
The Second Edition was published 23 July 2010.
The First Edition published 17 September 2009.

Morten Bergsmo (editor):
Criteria for Prioritizing and Selecting Core International Crimes Cases
Torkel Opsahl Academic EPublisher
Oslo, 2010
FICHL Publication Series No. 4 (Second Edition, 2010)
ISBN 978-82-93081-06-7
The Second Edition was published 23 July 2010
The First Edition was published 26 March 2009.

Morten Bergsmo and Pablo Kalmanovitz (editors):
Law in Peace Negotiations
Torkel Opsahl Academic EPublisher
Oslo, 2010
FICHL Publication Series No. 5 (Second Edition, 2010)
ISBN 978-82-93081-08-1
The Second Edition was published 23 July 2010.
The First Edition was published 26 March 2009.

Morten Bergsmo, César Rodríguez Garavito, Pablo Kalmanovitz and Maria Paula Saffon (editors):
Distributive Justice in Transitions
Torkel Opsahl Academic EPublisher
Oslo, 2010
FICHL Publication Series No. 6 (2010)
ISBN 978-82-93081-12-8
First published 23 July 2010.

Morten Bergsmo (editor):
Complementarity and the Exercise of Universal Jurisdiction for Core International Crimes
Torkel Opsahl Academic EPublisher
Oslo, 2010
FICHL Publication Series No. 7 (2010)
ISBN 978-82-93081-14-2
First published 23 July 2010

Morten Bergsmo (editor):
Abbreviated Criminal Procedures for Core International Crimes
Torkel Opsahl Academic EPublisher
Oslo, 2010
FICHL Publication Series No. 9 (2010)
ISBN 978-82-93081-20-3
First published 23 July 2010

All volumes are freely available as e-books on the FICHL homepage www.fichl.org. Paper copies may be ordered online at www.amazon.co.uk.

NOTES:

www.ingramcontent.com/pod-product-compliance
Lightning Source LLC
Chambersburg PA
CBHW071358230926
51846CB00002B/593
* 9 7 8 8 2 9 3 0 8 1 0 0 5 *